BIRDS OF DAYBREAK

Frances Bickford
Museum of New Mexico Gift Shop
Sept. 17, 1990   Santa Fe

BIRDS OF DAYBREAK

Landscapes and Elegies

Poetry by
Peggy Pond Church

William Gannon
Santa Fe, New Mexico
1985

Copyright ©1985 by Peggy Pond Church

All rights reserved including the right to reproduce this book in any form.

ISBN 0-88307-664-0

Library of Congress Catalog Card Number 84-82440

Address all orders and inquiries to:

William Gannon, Publisher
143 Sombrio Drive
Santa Fe, NM 87501

Book design by Virginia Gannon.

Cover drawing inspired by Mimbres pottery designs.

Photo of author on back cover ©Copyright 1984 by Cynthia Farah.

Grateful acknowledgement is made to The Arts in Psychotherapy: An International Journal *for permission to reprint "Stones On An Arid Hillside," which was first published by them in 1982.*

"Morning On Tshirege" *was first published in* Ultimatum for Man *in 1946.*

"A Lament On Tsankawi Mesa" *was first published by the Thistle Press in 1980.*

"Elegy For A Cacique's Daughter" *first appeared in* Selected Poems 1930-1982, *a cassette tape recorded in 1982.*

"White Dog With Mushrooms" *was first published in* New & Selected Poems *by Ahsahta Press in 1976.*

"For a Mountain Burial" *was first published in* The Friends *Bulletin in 1984.*

BIRDS OF DAYBREAK

Landscapes and Elegies

Poetry by
Peggy Pond Church

William Gannon
Santa Fe, New Mexico
1985

Copyright ©1985 by Peggy Pond Church

All rights reserved including the right to reproduce this book in any form.

ISBN 0-88307-664-0

Library of Congress Catalog Card Number 84-82440

Address all orders and inquiries to:

William Gannon, Publisher
143 Sombrio Drive
Santa Fe, NM 87501

Book design by Virginia Gannon.

Cover drawing inspired by Mimbres pottery designs.

Photo of author on back cover ©Copyright 1984 by Cynthia Farah.

Grateful acknowledgement is made to The Arts in Psychotherapy: An International Journal *for permission to reprint "Stones On An Arid Hillside," which was first published by them in 1982.*

"Morning On Tshirege" was first published in Ultimatum for Man *in 1946.*

"A Lament On Tsankawi Mesa" was first published by the Thistle Press in 1980.

"Elegy For A Cacique's Daughter" first appeared in Selected Poems 1930-1982, *a cassette tape recorded in 1982.*

"White Dog With Mushrooms" was first published in New & Selected Poems *by Ahsahta Press in 1976.*

"For a Mountain Burial" was first published in The Friends *Bulletin in 1984.*

CONTENTS

MORNING ON TSHIREGE   9
SANDHILL CRANES IN FEBRUARY   11
STONES ON AN ARID HILLSIDE   13
BLACK MESA: DREAM AND VARIATIONS   15
THE RITO: FRIJOLES CANYON   19
A LAMENT ON TSANKAWI MESA   25
ELEGY FOR A CACIQUE'S DAUGHTER   29
IN MEMORIAM: FSC 1900-1975   33
RETURN TO A LANDSCAPE   35

ON THE PUTTING TO DEATH OF AN OLD DOG   45
ROADSIDE MUSEUM   48
ENDANGERED SPECIES   51
WHITE DOG WITH MUSHROOMS   53
ELEGY FOR THE WILLOW TREE   55
A MEMORY OF HORSES   57

ODE FOR A SUMMER DAY   61
LINES FOR A GRANDDAUGHTER, AGE TWENTY   65
PERHAPS IN OUR OLD AGE   67
CONVOCATION OF BLUEBIRDS   68
THE KITES AND THE PETROGLYPHS   69
FOR A MOUNTAIN BURIAL   71

To the memory of my husband, Ferm Church, who shared with me fifty years of clouds and stones and desert rivers.

MORNING ON TSHIREGE

When I was a child I climbed here
at sunrise, barefooted among the grasses.
I searched for arrowheads among the ruins
and stood wondering on the rims of the broken kivas.
I had no language to say what it was that moved me,
a wisdom of rocks and old trees, of buried rivers,
of the great arcs and tangents of sky and mountain,
and always the grass that whispered upon the ruins
where a people had lived and fought,
had died and had been forgotten.

They had left drawn on the rocks their suns, their serpents,
and scattered among the dust the broken potsherds
with their symbols of cloud, of rain, of the eagle flying.
And so without words I knew that man is mortal
and doomed both to live and to die, but what he worships
lives on forever.

Today with my own world crumbling toward ruin
I know this still, and I greet the child who will stand here
upon Tshirege and watch the morning blossom
and feel under her questioning hand the living grasses
weaving substance of sunlight and the dust of a fallen city.

SANDHILL CRANES IN FEBRUARY

And on and on they came
through the pale afternoon,
long strands and ribbons,
arcs and curving wedges,
hieroglyphs in motion,
staves of music.

We looked upward again and again and saw them flying
and as they flew they called to one another;
the call sounded
through those myriad throats like the voice of a single being
half angel and half bird;
a wind sound, a water sound,
a sound as golden as honey.
We listened and felt ourselves enchanted
beyond our mortal sense.

All afternoon the sky was our dancing ground.
The long song rose and fell.
The convergent lines formed circles.
We were children again in a ring around a rosy
immersed in a mystery.
In the end we must all fall down
and down
in a slow spiral out of heaven
and be ourselves again.

Earth and our stolid bodies claimed us.
We leaned against stones.
The white clouds were slate clean.
On either side the cliffs were voiceless sandstone.
All afternoon the cranes kept flying over
aligning themselves with music.

As the sound ebbed we spoke wistfully of dying,
when our time came, into such ecstasy.

STONES ON AN ARID HILLSIDE

Stones that lie scattered on an arid hillside
longing for beauty in the eye of the beholder;
there are rainbows in them
waiting for definition,
dance figures, ritual intentions.

A stone cannot move by itself
yet something in it delights in motion,
to roll down a steep slope,
to be carried somewhere by water,
to migrate in great companies as birds do.

Perhaps stones are a motion picture
slowed down to the point of immobility.
If the film could be speeded up
what a tremendous onrush:
a stampede of stones hurling themselves toward ocean
dragging rivers along behind them.

Stones only seem motionless
because my mind cannot keep up with their gyrations.
If I hold one long enough
the atoms will start whirling;
the cold stone warms;
I feel it throb in my hand like a caught bird or a secret.

"God's activity is not the same in a man as in a stone,"
says Meister Eckhart.
I tremble to think of the god's activity,
the lines of force that meet here,
earth's weight, the moon's rhythmical attraction;
the essence of time compacted in such small mass.
The stone is not mortal yet there is a spirit in it;
it absorbs light.
When it becomes dust it too will someday feed roots.

"When attention is directed to the idea of a stone
the idea of an angel cannot be entertained,"
says Eckhart
with the smile of an old Zen master.
I find I cannot think of one without the other.
A stone is more enigmatic than an angel.
I ask it questions;
it answers me in riddles.
I read it like the palm of my hand.
What if it were a fragment of a god's hand,
a fingerprint,
undeniable evidence?
Among thousands and thousands
how long will it be before I find the right one?

I keep thinking the markings in stones
are like grooves of music
that could be played if only I knew how,
if only I had the right instrument,
the correct equation,
a sense more skillful than my blind ear.
Suppose each stone were packed full of sound
as a computer's memory—
If I pressed the right key
would I hear the crystals growing?
Would colors be audible?
Would the stones call out to one another,
each in its own mineral language?
If I could learn how to listen
would I someday hear the stone's voice
that goes on and on putting God into its own words?

BLACK MESA: Dream and Variations

I.

In a twilight of rain
the mesa gathered her robes around her,
veils of mauve and blown smoke,
colors of dark cloud lined with a buried sunset.

The mountain, the Black Mesa,
loomed suddenly before us like a ghost ship,
a figment of clouds and torn sails
gone aground out of time,
cast up out of a never-existing ocean.
No seacoast welcomed her,
only the bare hills and a desert river.
What resonance of waters,
what urge in clouds and in stone to take form
in a reflecting eye had seized us
to be its collaborators?
The Black Mesa
waked an old legend in us, tales of a black ship
or a ship with black sails we could only half remember,
an alien dream projected from a past world
through our rapt eyes
on the curtain of rain and darkness.

II.

On this afternoon of vision
they were dancing the Turtle Dance at San Ildefonso
in a medley
of shells and green boughs.
Left alone
for an hour on the other side of the river,
closed in by a slow rain,
I slept in the labyrinth of myself.
I went down through the vertical corridors of heaped time
with their indelible graffiti,
their coiled and unascended music,

down to the melt of the world and the unformed crystal essence
that would someday blossom and reflect light.
I listened at the root of the Black Mesa
like an attached child
that hears only its own and its mother's heartbeat.

III.

The mesa,
alert to the sound of the drum and of strung shells,
of ascending male voices,
guarded her mystery
in cinders and slow crystals,
in a mantle of river stones,
in the sloped debris of worn hills,
in facets of retained light.

Monument to earth's fire,
the melt of her inwardness:
unnamed gods came surging
forth from the womb's dark.
Taking light in their hands as they rose
they wove it like a vestment
over hills wrinkled with time,
over stones long abandoned by their rivers.

IV.

Landmarked center of a universe,
terrestrial axis,
still body at the center of time's motion,
I have watched morning and evening revolve around you,
heard the seasonal birds fly over,
handled the washed stones,
looked down on you from the stretched rim of mountains
at the valley's either side.
Always you drew my wandering gaze toward you
from whatever height I leaned on.
From each direction I saw the light drain downward
seeking to fill your dark well.

You are a lodestone,
compact essence of extinct fire,
a hand reaching
out of earth's whirling depth to seize light
and make yourself its darker habitation.

V.

Black Mesa,
hard core from which a landscape
has been eaten away by rainfall and a river.
Washed gravels at rest above earth's tilt
lie level as instruments among the torn hills,
anatomy of an island or an altar.
Oceans of light wash round her.
The Black Mesa devours light
like a collapsed star,
drawing it down into the dark shaft
from which her substance fountained.
Leaning columns of black rock
intrude shadow
like bars of upright music.
Only the pale grass at the surface shines
softly in winter,
a platform raised for the feet of holy dancers.

VI.

The river levels the land around the mesa.
Sleek as an animal, muscular as serpents,
it is bearing our world away.

The river's aim is only to flow onward;
the mesa's to remain.
Among the stars and seasons
she keeps her fixed place.
Though the earth moves beneath her,
 though the mountains perish,
 she is rooted too deep to tremble.
She has been through it all before.
She will still be here when the hills crumble
and are heaped along a no longer living
river.
When the drums fall silent
who will they be who someday come to dream her
into themselves again?

THE RITO: *Frijoles Canyon*

I.

Midday:
the canyon brimming with green fragrance.
The stream has been running with her clear eyes bandaged,
heaving a burden of ash
from last summer's fire-ruined forest;
strives toward transparency,
tears at her banks and heals them.

The canyon is a green island.
The stream has carved it
out of a ruin of dust heaved from a volcano;
millenniums of time for this small, patient,
slowly unwinding thread of water
to pierce its way down through black lavas,
a chaos of rolled rock,
rough ledges and pinnacles,
a furious architecture,
seasons of ice and winter,
seasons of summer and burst clouds.

This little river
somehow stays virginal;
returns to her pure and constant being,
forever changeless in change.
                        Here,
yet forever passing onward.

II.

A young girl on the verge of puberty
leaves a boisterous family of picnickers
as though the murmurous water had enticed her
into some secret world.
She tests the current with her bare feet
and finds it too chill for wading,

draws back a little, then continues her exploration;
feels pebbles, feels the fine sand.
Her toes are agile and confident.
They long perhaps to become fishes
or at least webbed as frogs are.
She curls them round the surface of a
half submerged tree branch,
extends her body
in a ballet dancer's position,
left leg horizontal,
arms reaching forward;
over and over achieves delighted balance.
She does not smile.
She is practicing a lesson,
intent as though the voice of the stream were teaching
her the grace of its own movement.

III.

The trees close to the river
are lithe and smooth-limbed as she.
Farther back
on the pine-needled floor of the canyon
the older trees are bark-encrusted,
thickened with age and achieved life.
Lightning has scarred them.
The weight of storms has twisted
some of them slantwise;
yet time has not overwhelmed them.
Reaching tall toward the light
they keep shedding their outgrown branches.
They rise like pillars as though from under water
into the sky's blue element.
Their crowns stir slowly in the least wind.

IV.

At midday the canyon swarms with picnickers
for whom silence has always seemed a strange word.
They shout and scramble,
play games,
wander on strict paths among the ruins.

Cautious tour guides
watch over and inform them,
share crusts of knowledge,
repeat for them the names of birds and branches,
tell them they must not touch,
point warningly to ladders
that lead upward to a desecrated kiva.
Ancestral spirits have long since fled this precinct,
leaving no trace in the worn dust.

Children who never learned here
to make prayer feathers,
to greet the sun at daybreak,
to coil clay in the laughing presence of their mothers,
how can they know what the canyon itself would teach them
growing up in the rhythm of its seasons?
What animal voice will bless them?
What cloud will blossom,
will scatter its rain and its lightnings at their summons?

V.

And yet the essence of those long past seasons lingers
everywhere in this canyon,
traces of memory
imbedded in leaf, in stone,
in the ripple of water
flashing by us
yet never gone.

The stream, the maiden,
releases herself from darkness, from the heaped snows,
comes singing her wintry way under pale ice,
unwinds in summer through a brushy tangle
of alder and willow,
glides sinuous under
low apricot-colored ledges.

Now like a bridled filly abandons her wild ways,
becomes docile and domestic,
flows in slow curves among grasses,

glitters in sunlight where the canyon widens,
where cornfields in their time replaced the wild rose,
where children once laughed and played in the lively water.
Their mothers, watching, spoke a gentle language
half ripple and half bird song.

The little stream, the *rito*,
listened,
received into her motion
mourning and merriment,
reflected dreams and visions
that shone above her in the eyes of humans;
unaltered in herself kept flowing onward,
half monster and half music;
for time's brief moment here knew gentleness,
freed of her serpent skin.

VI.

I sit here with my old friend remembering years when
the trail to the canyon was narrow. Whoever came here
walked down it as though into another
world or even into
another dimension of time
or of themselves.
Who knows what we sought?
a return to a past not ours?
an escape?
a revelation?
What was it that had called us
each one to the sharp brink of this wilderness
and bade us enter here if we were worthy
of time's transfigurations?
Imagined or real there was something that renewed us
like an ancient wellspring or a legend.

The canyon embraced us as part of its own being;
heard through our ears the ripple and cadence of the river,
the mourning dove's slow croon,
the wild turkey's warning
call like a row of struck bells.
Evening till daybreak the stir of invisible creatures,

a rustle, a soft padding, a twig broken,
shadows that fled across moonlight,
moonlight a substance
that spread like a tide, creating islands,
inlets and coves, an archipelago
past which only the stars sailed.

VII.

How long ago that was.
The stars retreat farther each year. Human chatter
scrawls jagged lines across the face of silence.
The new road now brings thousands
who do not know what roots are
or the seasons of ripening.

"I wonder who else has seen so many changes?"
my old friend sighs, she for whom the canyon
has been home for nearly a lifetime.
We who spent our young days
among the mounds and shards of a vanished people
must count ourselves now among the vanishing.
What we remember
cannot live after us.
We smile at one another
as though the present were a dream around us.
Within us the canyon and the still melodious river
lead a secret life that only we can enter.

Coda

Autumn –
The golden leaves whirl downward
spicing the canyon floor.
The wedge of blue air upholds each leaf like a dancer
loosed from her partner's hand.
The leaves fall lightly
upon the withering grass.
They drift on the brown water,
then settle slowly among roots and grasses
into the stream whose motion scarcely moves them.

A LAMENT ON TSANKAWI MESA

(The Tewa name "Tsankawi" means "pueblo ruin at the gap of the sharp round cactus." It was inhabited approximately from A.D. 1200-1600.)

I.

On the rough slope of Tsankawi
mesa among the ledges of windbitten rock,
vestigial caverns that
a dwarf race might once have inhabited,
I imagine a hand-small population
that only playing children would have been aware of;
even the trees are dwarf size.
A knee-high scrub oak
surprises me with the rose-red color of its new leaves
against an arid rock.
I wonder at the power of the blind root
to pierce its way upward
on the trail of mineral dissolution,
minerals coughed up
from a volcano's angry heart,
earth's blood hardened
the color of a sacrifice or a sunset.

II.

The south slope of this mesa
is for me the next thing to a moonscape,
sun-beaten, water-deprived;
rock breaks off in raw chunks
as though wedge-split
lies tumbled, resisting erosion;
foot-trails once were smooth grooves
worn by bare feet or sandals
that polished as they trod.
Now our own heavy footfall
has widened the trails and scraped them open;
the soft bone of earth is powdered;
the gone years crumble;
the masked figures, unlistening,
fade into the rock face.

III.

Press now
through the scarred gap of the sharp round cactus,
sheered cleft in the rock rim;
climb by the broken footholds
as though from a nether world
upward like first man on the Ladder of Emergence,
upward out of the earth wombs.
What is it in me or what in the rock remembers
an ancient ritual,
sound of a far drum,
a flutter of shells at the knee,
a swing of feathers and fox fur?

The Sky Gods begin to take shape.
The floor of the earth is lifted
like an island above the broken canyons.
Light breaks in long waves against the cliff forms,
a sea of light welling upward out of the valley,
an illusion of great height; yet
the eagle soars above me,
his motion creating silence.

IV.

And here
where only the gods should walk
a pueblo ruin,
stone fallen upon stones.
Weeds and rough grasses
feed on their own decay, grow rampant
out of the roofless kivas;
only the red ants
build and rebuild their conical palaces
destroyed by the harsh tread of unheeding humans.

V.

I remember how years and years ago I rode here,
finding my way from the lower slopes of the mesa,
a more gradual ascent, and letting my mare graze
among the grassy stones;
wandered alone upon the collapsed walls

and heard stir
echoes across time of human voices,
a tinkle of laughter as though invisible forms were watching
alert as the bright-eyed lizards.

Now nothing but silence.

Not like the fulfilled silence after music.
Silence complete and dead
like a dead animal
that once ran quick with life.
Even the wind's sound
cannot erase such silence,
a silence out of which long ago the gods spoke,
through which men's feathered prayers were wafted,
studded with birdcalls,
resonant with color,
now blank as an eye in which light is no longer moving.

VI.

What has changed?

Is it I who have changed?

The light-footed child I was no longer answers;
the exuberant life has dwindled,
no longer lifts me
feather-blown above earth's weight.
The waters invoked once
with reverence from the furled cloud
are no longer being replenished,
fade now from a surge to a trickle,
a stain, a dampness only in the channel,
as though the springs were flowing now too slowly
to clear themselves of earth's darkness.
The steep rock steps that used to lift me
upward
now weigh on me like a burden.

Is it I who have changed
or has time changed within me?
Giant machines with an evil eye
spread themselves over the mesas;
the expended waters run useless
in a venomous plume out of Mortendad Canyon.
On Tsankawi
I no longer hear even a distant echo
of the drum that once called Awanyu.

VII.

I cannot call back that solitude, that living silence,
yet the scrub oak still unfurls its delicate
spring leaves;
an inconspicuous daisy, small as an eyelid,
blossoms in white clusters near the scarred trail,
puccoon lifts yellow salvers filled with nectar
distilled out of driest dust.

On the surface of the mesa
where the once-molten rock is stone hard,
dwarf cacti flourish their water-lily blossoms
like a half dreamt mirage. A scarlet paintbrush
splashes sudden red out of the thin soil;
pottery fragments
sing broken phrases of lost music.

Perhaps I was wrong after all about the silence.

Perhaps if I stand here alone and listening
I can hear time work through and within me.
Roots extract poison and honey from the same rock;
forms of unborn music
wait here to be transmuted.

The grey-green lichen takes the world apart
and we do not shudder at it.

ELEGY FOR A CACIQUE'S DAUGHTER

I.

Cleaning my house I keep thinking of you, Reycita,
sick now in hospital,
perhaps mortally sick,
and no way of getting through to help you
if an alien love could help.
Indian, grandmother, abandoned wife,
clung to by indulged sons,
you have worked your fingers into hard knots
cleaning other people's houses,
furnishing your own with castoffs
and shoddy appliances,
the crusts left over after installment purchase.

As I scrub my floor I think of how you scrubbed it
the last time. It seems as though you were still here,
your quiet hands at the sink
washing and polishing.
You look up now and then
with pride and uncertainty
for my approval.
Who am I to approve you,
oh daughter of a cacique, daughter of prayerful men?
We both know
what it is to be proud of our households,
to be proud of the woman in ourselves,
keeping each our share of our separate worlds
in order.

We used to talk women's ways with one another,
of sons and of sons' deaths,
of deaths and disappointments,
the plight of men not finding a way to become men
in the kind of world ours is now.
We were both baffled by the world's confusion.
The roads that were once clear
led each into wilderness
though different for us both.

We compared notes with one another
and knew the times that had lived us
would not return again.

II.

Reycita, Reycita,
I hold you to me
as though I shared your death struggle,
you my servant
on Tuesdays for almost a year now.
I am living your death as you die it
alone in hospital, speechless,
guarded by strangers,
by cold electronic devices —
no one to hold your clenched hand,
to smooth your forehead,
no voice you have known,
no remembered language.
Reycita, my servant,
my sister in the task of being woman.

As though something within me
envied the reality of your life,
as though I held a smooth pot in my hand
shaped in an ancient time.
All my strictness, my avarice,
possessions and books and comforts
shame me before you.
They are the weight I carry,
worth nothing now
in this wordless confrontation.
I do not know what lies behind your locked eyes.

III.

She tells me, our mutual friend,
how she too has been aware of your daily presence
about her listening house.
You have not yet been given your leave to die.

They are keeping your body living
as though this were all that mattered —
the flesh, the heaving lung,
the sluggish fluids.
Yet while they chain you
like a dumb prisoner to this world
I feel sure by your presence in our hearts,
you have escaped them;
your spirit has escaped.
You visit with gentle humor
among those whom you served once,
content to renew the familiar tasks of women,
our menial work,
to find your joy in ours.

IV.

We bid you godspeed, Reycita,
we who keep watch for you,
near, or at a distance.
May your spirit go free of these fetters,
the intricate technology that resists death:
tubes, the mouth opened in the throat
that forces you to keep breathing,
the fluids dripped nasally
into your mindless blood,
the mind itself gone blank behind the eyelids.
May there be no more bad dreams,
no daily anxiety,
the struggle to live,
and to keep your children living,
grown men that they are who have
married women not worth you.

I knew your longing
somehow at last to be able to live your own life
in your own separate way,
not as mother, nor mother-in-law,
not sister, nor daily servant,
but true, true to your life's accumulated wisdom
and the wholeness of your own heart.

V.

Go in peace now, Reycita.
Escape those who watch,
who would steal you from death, contriving
nets and snares to impede the vanished spirit.
Go as breath-feather blown over the blue mountains
to the realm of the Ancestors.
Be cloud.
Be rain.
Be earth. Be flowing water.
Be the wings of summer birds.

IN MEMORIAM
FSC
1900-1975

Yesterday we scattered your ashes
on the ash strewn slope of a volcanic canyon
among the sparse green shrubs
and the dark shards of cooking pots broken
who knows how long ago?
Yet the presence of those vanished people lingers
everywhere as though their footprints
were still warm from another time.

We too
once called a nearby mesa home.
We knew its weathers:
how the clouds surged like waves
and released their lightnings;
how the snow blew down in a whisper among the pine trees;
the tracks that furred animals made in winter;
the patterned brilliance of starlight.

We knew which mountains were sacred;
the male and the female rains;
the life-givingness of water.
We were aware of an essence, a nameless spirit
wherever the gods of humans have been honored:
something that does not die,
only changes, perhaps, its mode of being
as we must our mode of seeing.

I remember how you and I sat together
far up this talus on almost our last picnic.
How silent you were.
How you gazed without once speaking
beyond the canyon's mouth and over the light-drenched valley
to the mountains that were so long our shared horizon.
Were the landmarks already becoming unfamiliar?
Had you gone so far already on your last journey
that your thought by now was speaking a different language?

The sound of wind in the pines was always your favorite music.
As we scattered your ashes the wind lifted some of them in a light cloud;
the rest mingled instantly with the weathered fragments
of volcanic ash at the cliff's base.
On the way down among the anonymous grasses
one of us found an arrowhead,
obsidian, perfect in shape,
a word joining then with now
and all our own past with forever.

RETURN TO A LANDSCAPE

for Mary McArthur Bryan

I.

Around the mountain,
backward into a world behind time,
landscape expanding like a dream,
like rings that widen and vanish across water.

All this world had been water once
and mountains crumbled,
washed down to form plains that still hold the form of water,
hills rounded and rippled like a moving ocean,
grass in the wind making the motion of water.
Ahead of us black ridges like a seacoast
where the tides of wind race upward
and shatter against the unswerving walls of black rock,
black rock that was fluid once
and retains the sharp memory of fire.

Oh these are plains
that summon something like music to a man's blood,
a surge, a deep-sea swelling.
Doors open within him on a far space
broken only by morning and evening.
A feeling of wildness
knocks at his unaccustomed heart.
It is as though a released bird
remembered the use of wings.
The sloping grasslands
waken ancient nomadic dreams.
Visions of grazing herds begin to shimmer;
the horseman wakens;
a sudden rhythm of riding
pulses at wrists and knees.
Oh limitless space! Oh brightness
of clear air!

Out of the youth leaps a manhood
like the sword from encasing stone.
A new land awaits him with its unborn legends,
its challenge, its trials of strength.
He has bidden his fathers farewell.
The voices of cautionary women
call after him ever more faintly and without answer.

Born of such men, you and I,
exuberant children
whose fathers, half in playfulness, half earnest,
put bridles into our hands and taught us to gallop
with the wind and the sun and the power of a strong horse running;
taught us before we knew writing and spelling
to clasp the leather saddle with our firm knees,
to speak with our hands through relaxed reins,
to feel the animal's spirit part ours
and ours the horizon-seeking mind that was wholly human.

Now we, two aging women,
wrenched from this land before our youth was over,
still feel the imprint of its seasons
like rings that mark a tree's growth.
Strangers to one another through half our lifetime
we share no kinship,
no ancestral memories unite us
yet
closer than kinship
the current of earth's music that flows through us.
At the end of our separate pilgrimage
we come together in time's single focus
and mingle our memories.

It is these men, our fathers, whose blood moves in us,
old women that we now are.
We who have borne our own children
and seen them grown and gone,
stand here at the rim of our spent childhood
when we were still half-girl, half-boy.
Woman's strict destiny had not claimed us;
distance enchanted us;
rough trails like an unspoken language

were ours to decipher daily:
this way the shod or the cleft hoof
passed, the print of the predator
crossed here. Above us the storm clouds
threatened and drove us at a gallop
ahead of rainfall back to safe roofs and our warm walls,
back to the rancher's homeplace
that for children was all joy.
We knew nothing then of its difficult dimension,
the wrestling with losses and dry seasons,
maternal terrors,
a woman's troubled dreams of her children's future
and the long loneliness.

The women, my mother and yours,
endured for the men's sake.
They quieted themselves with gardens and with sewing.
I still wear my mother's silver thimble
that was her grandmother's before;
when I prick my finger
the drop of blood is theirs.

My mother sewed flowered curtains
to make her room a bower.
She made no concession at all to wilderness.
Would not meet it even halfway —
she who in childhood rode her grandfather's tall horses,
the least motion of her hands exacting obedience.
Her childhood love of wildness withered in her,
a promise blighted
before the too early blossom could set fruit.
I think she never
forgave the uncaring land.

How did we come by our unmothered love of bare hills
that grew strong in our lives like a wide-spreading tree
outweathering all our weathers?
What stirring of once known springs and waters
urges us to return like birds that migrate
in response to a slant of light?
We wandered all day on roads that only you remembered,
yet familiar as my own dreams.

II.

Toward the end of the glowing afternoon
we came to the cemetery
half an unplanted mile past the waning town.
The dark bulk of the Wagonmound shelters it,
a shape imagined
in the light-dazed eyes of waterless travelers.
Now the lapsed tides of history have left it stranded
like the wraith of a beached ship.
Only the dust long years ago compacted
by the struggling wagonwheels remembers,
and the bones of the dead who lived in the shadow of its legend.

"That cemetery that wants to be a poem," my notes say,
"from Greek *Kometerion*, a sleeping place":
a sleeping place out of doors
as though trail-weary travelers
had thrown their blankets down on the bare earth
and made the sky their roof —
a long night watch
and the bright familiar stars;
by day the striding sun,
cloud shadows, rainfall,
herds in far distance moving,
an eagle in rings of flight.

The dead are resting here in weathered silence.
The same grass waves over them that waves on the plain beyond;
the feathered seed stems
are printed on light like the notes of composed music,
a score waiting the wind's touch.
Unswayed by any wind the marble gravestones
defy mortality. More resistant to time than mountains
they will become dust
long after the shape of the Wagonmound is forgotten.
The polished gray surfaces
do not blend with the sloped land;
their squared shapes are dissonant.
Light flows around them
like waves around tidal markers.

As we stand together by your father's graveplot
the high winds of autumn blow over us.
Far off the cattle herds are moving
to their seasonal destination.
Cloud shadows scud
across the rippled hills.

Like children studying a primer
we lean closer to read the straight-ruled biographies
imprinted on each stone:
a name, a birthdate, the year in which a life ended;
a few curt numbers,
all that remain to mark the little space
in measureless time these lives filled.
Your father died too young, still in achieving midlife
when his children were not half grown.
Much later your mother returned to lie beside him
in final companionship;
nothing to tell of how they lived together,
endured the land or loved it.

The home ranch
has passed into other hands.
No one of your name now
rides the long fences or
counts the drifting lines of cattle or
watches the sky for blessing or threat of rainfall.
Only this narrowed space of earth remains
out of all he once called his own —
all that had once seemed yours
as in childhood my father's acres
seemed mine, my storybook, my
horizon-bounded playground.
Today I envied your heritage
of this little length of ground,
your right, when you die, to be part of it
which perhaps you will never claim.

Why does it seem to matter
to some of us, I wonder,
with what dust our bones are mingled?
Your father sleeps here
with his life absorbed into the land's silence;

mine far away in the city he thought he had escaped from.
It was a possessive sister
who on his death retrieved the prodigal
and consigned his reluctant ashes to the cold tomb.
Did the released spirit, I wonder,
find its own way back among the lights and shadows
to the high plains he loved?
without bones or mortal body
to be borne as in dream to the place of his dream's emergence?

Women have seen men lose their hearts to landscape.
My father did; and yours, more fortunate,
won a livelihood. In death he was not exiled.
The woman beside him, your mother,
would have preferred to lie at the roots of roses
with a green lawn over her.
What can she do with so much empty space,
no great trees to cast shadow
between her and the naked sun?

My own mother
grew intolerant of wide vistas.
After my father's death she built a new house with high windows
and shut the mountain out.
She who in her school days played Rosalind
let Rosalind die in her, denied the forest
and armored herself in duty.
She hid the gypsy girl's wistful picture
and no longer sang us ballads.

Sometimes I remember
with a pang in my heart how she once tried to teach me
in a brimming darkness edged with pine trees
the names of the bright stars and the constellations,
the Lyre, the Swan, the Sword of Perseus.
For her the night sky gleamed with heroes.
The horseman she married ran away from dragons.
After the children came he insisted on remaining
only a laughing child still.
He used the land for his plaything. She became housebound.
The swift-footed mare he gave her was never again saddled.

I, her firstborn,
molded feature on feature in her own likeness,
grew up with a different nature.
The first air I breathed was the midnight air of a canyon
cleft in these same wide plains.
Wherever I went I carried its imprint in me
as the fish to deep water the mark of its spawning ground.
When I die I would like to return to this earth that made me
and be part once more of its substance,
the smallest crystal
that still holds the memory of a human lifetime
in minute circuitry. Whatever my reaching senses
have touched
becomes one with the resonance of rock,
with the underground whisper of sunken waters,
with magnetic currents
that roots and the smallest insects are aware of.
I carry a cell in which all I have seen lies folded,
mountains and oceans and storm clouds,
mineral color and the color of light reflected
in stone and in waterdrop.
The air I have breathed will someday be shaped into another music.

As I stood beside you in the graveyard
I felt memory throb within us.
Our young days were not lost.
The life we had taken hold of
was conformed to the shape of our hands;
in each whorl of a fingertip,
each braided line of our palms, the feel of our lives still lingered.
Our eyes have netted this land with lines of beauty.
Whatever once stirred in us will go on singing.

Do the dead, I wonder, listen?
Does an essence linger
that is sentient still to music?
Will the grass springing over us absorb our dreaming
and scatter it among birdcalls?

ON THE PUTTING TO DEATH OF AN OLD DOG

Put to death:
The words we used were
"put to sleep,"
but sleep is not the same thing
as death.
In sleep the breath comes and goes still.
Under the eyelids dreams flicker;
the paws twitch
at intervals with a running motion.
When I watched you sleeping near me
I knew that life was living in you.
Your senses would vibrate in dreaming
like the tuned strings of an instrument.
Your still form stretched out
was filled with some purpose
remote from my human world.
It was as though you traveled
trails you had never seen
yet familiar as you dreamed them.
Did the arctic wastes of your origin
wake in you?
Did you follow the scent, perhaps,
of a snowshoe rabbit
through a far white winter landscape?
You were running free of the leash now,
free of the restraining world of humans.

I recall how on the trail when I rested
you would come to my side a moment
and then withdraw
to contemplate wilderness after your own fashion,
ears sifting the air for the least rustle
of bird's wing or of insect,
nose sniffing the language of worlds I could not enter.
When I slept in the noon shade you would roam a little
but never too far.
Something bound you to me
stronger than wild ancestral yearnings.
I forced you to obey me,
to keep your place always,

to suppress your exuberance
for the sake of domestic calm;
yet your leaps of wild ecstasy
stirred Dionysos in my own blood.
Sometimes by mountain water
I would feel my heart start beating
to the sound of a long forgotten music.

When you grew old
and your senses were fast failing
the veterinary surgeon
put you to sleep
and death.
It was a simple operation.
I kept my hands on you all the time.
You could no longer hear me,
the voice of command, the voice of reassurance,
the voice of love
and at last of separation.
How often my words had calmed you on the same high table,
trembling as all dogs do
at the probing fingers,
the preventive inoculations.
It seemed strange
that this time you did not flinch when the anesthetic needle went in,
nor draw back when the tube like a slender serpent
found the vein through which death must enter.
It seemed as though you withdrew
of your own free will
and shut the last door between us.

For a moment you lay outstretched in your warm fur,
warm under my hands that rested on you,
warm as though sleeping near me on your house rug
or bedded in winter sunlight on the white snow:
then in one single instant
gone;
as though someone had thrown a master switch
and the world's machinery silenced,
no more light,
nothing that could receive warmth
from the touch of a warm hand.

The life surging through you, in one eye's blink
vanished
without a trace or an echo.
Whatever in you had dreamed
was gone too.
Nothing remained
but this complete cessation,
and I, an old woman, clutching at a dream's end
wordless in the steep shadow
of my own death.

ROADSIDE MUSEUM

On a Sunday afternoon in autumn
in a wide valley where
the earth had been torn open by
rain's rage, the cliffs bled
like a petrified sunset.
Mountains had been swallowed by rivers
alive and chewed small.
Grass grew
hardly where wind swept
leaf cover off too fast
to set soil.
The sun's hot heel
blistered the earth till it peeled up
in thin flakes the color of
charred flesh.

We stopped at a roadside museum where
travelers are enticed in
to study the natural history
of the region.
Quickly we found ourselves
in one of the lesser
but nonetheless painful circles
of what would once have been called hell.
In slick glass cases along the wall
and outside in tight square
pens with floors of slanting
concrete, a pan of water and
no shade but a cave at the back
we saw animals, live,
some confined singly,
a few paired.

None but the prairie dogs have earth to dig in,
and they, restrained below ground
by cement dikes
and by a low wall above
stand upright as we pass
and press clawed fingers
on the wall like old men
or women taken prisoner too late
to learn another language.

We dared not touch them,
fearing the rodent teeth, yet
something in us that cannot bear a wall
began to bleed a little
like a pulled scar.

A mouse-furred vole
rummages through his case,
his twisted eyes
finding no place to hide,
not the least wisp of shadow.
Clenched in the ball of himself
there is brief night;
but the furl will not hold
and the dizzy hunt keeps on.
Loose earth
cannot tunnel;
light's eye blazes
five-sided in a dream of claws
and talons.

The horned owl
tethered by one leg
on a patch of bare ground
as bare as Golgotha,
feathers and ear-tufts disheveled
like Lear in the tempest,
winces his golden eyes in the
drench of midday
and with a piteous motion
huddles against the
sharp and narrow shadow
of the smooth stake.
Oh may a dream of forest
branches and leaves be cool and woven
on the taut curtains of his closed eyes.

While
obscure in their dens as though
curled softly in safe wombs
the great cats

once sacred to goddesses
endure captivity like queens.
From the curve of a shoulder
or a yellow paw glimpsed
we reconstruct a pattern of constellations,
leonine beings
or the lynx whose face burns like a
thorn.
Pent in the grave of herself each lies still
as the failed ashes
of a spent fire.

But what whisper of
wisdom, I wonder,
inspires the coyote
lone in his pen to create for himself
a plaything?
As though he were fishing he
scoops bare water from his pen then
runs to chase
the moving stain on the concrete,
like a kitten with leaves
or mice.
This is imagination
which some say only in mankind
unmakes these prisons of flesh, of time
or of stone walls.

ENDANGERED SPECIES

For a Whooping Crane that Died of Poisoning from Lead Shot

There were only a hundred of them left
anywhere in the whole world
where once thousands in their migrations
crowded the night sky:
that long white river of high sound
uncoiled from the throats of birds.

Then man came
swarming over the continents:
fire in his hands;
falcons at his wrist;
a quiver full of arrows;
then guns mean and hard
sowing death like a mocking phallus.

Not content with extinguishing birds,
man takes arms against his own kind—
"— he who cannot bring one green leaf into being,"
an offended goddess said. "Somehow or other
mankind must be got rid of.
Since he has destroyed all other predators
I can do no more than let him
prey on himself till the last bone is stripped clean.
The weapons he has invented must destroy him.
Out of each violated atom he himself shall let loose
the fire of his own annihilation:

"After the fire, the darkness:
aeons of cold darkness.

"Perhaps then," said the goddess,
"I will once more smile upon the blind earth
and draw with the touch of my own skilled finger
a green cell out of the sea.
The green cell will start spinning the world again
from sunlight and long-unwakened water.
"In time there will be music
from the throats of birds and of angelic creatures
I have not yet begun to dream."

WHITE DOG WITH MUSHROOMS

On a smoothed-off hilltop
among the granite outcrops
I am sitting this December morning
observing among the random
and wrinkled stones at the base of a
juniper a colony of mushrooms
with caps the color of warm toast.

No bigger in circumference
than a dime and most of them
smaller, they are
gathered in clusters like a
game of jackstones,
or like stars on the sphere
of a child's eye.

The sky is pale blue; the wind
like an invisible herd with horns in velvet
goes butting among the rough trees.
My skin rejoices
in the warm prick of winter,
warmth and cold joined
like a pair of
lively dancers.

The white dog, Poli-kota,
runs on spiraling errands in her loose flesh.
She is a collector of footprints,
of urinal smells draped over
bushes and low tree branches.
Her curled tongue
delivers damp messages
to my cold cheek.

She is unmindful of mushrooms,
treads them down blindly
in a quadruple disaster.
My heart cries
to think what like death

may someday befall our planet,
not anyone's purpose,
no one will mean to do it,
something random to us
as Poli among the mushrooms.

Still
on this hillside
where dying and coming to life
go hand in hand together
I cannot mind long.

Here is a bone I have found,
perhaps a steer's vertebra
once hidden in gliding flesh.
Now weathered and whitened
it lies in my hand
like a wordless metaphor
in the shape of a butterfly.

ELEGY FOR THE WILLOW TREE

The willow tree in the garden
died back a little more each year.
Her long hair of green leaves,
each tear-shaped like the mark of a star on exposed film,
shortened and became thin.

She stood at the edge of the lawn like a witch in tatters
bereft of her youthful magic.
The knobs of her weathered bones showed through
and the cicatrices
of shed branches and amputations.
Her pose became awkward like that of an aged dancer
who can no longer keep up with the strong music
that summer and the winds weave.

I said to the man with the chain saw and the ladder,
"Let us now grant her a quick death.
Let the place where she stands be empty.
Let the birds take their song elsewhere.
Let us wipe our sky clean forever of this sad shape."

All afternoon I watched the branches falling
and winced in my deepest bone to hear the rough saw
cut through the rings of time.
Did those shudders, I wonder, spread downward among the clenched roots
and the choked-off fountains of dark water?
Did pain run quivering through earth's finest fibres?
Trembling I hid from the sound of that execution.

When I came out the green branches had been hauled off.
Only the rough trunk still stood
at the edge of the lawn like a monument.
A few handfuls of live green
were all that still trembled on the blank air.
And my heart wept for the lost golden presence,
for the circumference of shadow,
for the vertical strands of green music,
the long drooping arpeggios.

This tree was its own world.
It was alive with motion and with being.
Its leaves were a whirl of stars.
From now on what will the birds do?
the spiders who moored their webs here?
sunlight that traveled so far to become substance?

Oh what can I do to salvage a remnant of beauty
from beauty's dismemberment?
How can I tempt the rainbow
colors of summer to keep on dancing round her?
a wild clematis to wash its white stars over
like the froth of a blown wave?
or a thicket of aspen to lift a new green music
out of the rotted roots?

In time past my wish might have made a goddess of her
and hung the truncated form with offerings,
baskets of fruit and garlands, a cage of songbirds,
a harp out of Babylon.
Now I can only let her
go free to her un-becoming.
Under my feet the hungry earth is waiting
with its many-mouthed creatures to taste this sacrament.
Oh earth, air, water, fire!
Oh essence of bright summer!
I stand on the threshold of what mysteries?

A MEMORY OF HORSES

Do you still remember, little sister,
the horses we played among and dreamed of—
all one to us
whether sprung from imagination's quarry
or colted on summer grass?
We read *Black Beauty*
and that sleek and long-suffering
animal became our hero.
You named your pony
Black Beauty after him.
Then your Black Beauty died and you came to know too early
a child's inerasable grief,
blackness and beauty
paired forever after in your pierced heart.

My placid and gentle mare had been named Dolly
though certainly not by me; I would much have preferred
Flame Foot or Arabella.
In time I grew to love her.
When the mountain lion clawed her shoulder,
child though I was, they put me in charge of healing.
I learned to spread black ointment on her raw wound
so smoothly she did not flinch,
and kept the flies off
walking beside her all day along the streambank.
When her young colt
deserted the teat now and then to suckle at my finger
some imprint of motherhood stirred in me
whose breasts were not yet grown;
deeper within me
the thrust of poetry.
When she grazed by the spring among violets and willows
my scrawny mare was transfigured.
Then I found myself pretending
I had caught Pegasus with a magic bridle.

Neither of us could bear to see our horses shut up
in a tight-barred corral. One day we cut the check-rein
on Chili the stallion's harness
so his wild head could toss and swing free.
For once our father did not burn us with his anger.

He knew our hearts were tender;
so was his own, but discipline was his first rule
with children or animals.

We expected a spanking.
Instead he seated us beside him
on a sweet-smelling hay bale
and talked as though he thought we were reasonable beings.
The purpose of check-reins, he told us,
was not, as we thought, to hold the stallion's head up
for the sake of its owner's pride
but to give it security.
How we strained our hearts to believe him!

Nevertheless we went on pitying horses
that had to be caught and tamed.
For a long time we could not be cured of dreaming
of the wild stallion they talked of who never could be captured,
who came down from the mesas one night and kicked the corral rails
loose and led his imprisoned mares back to their freedom.
Sometimes even now I seem to hear the
ringing of those dark hooves. The imprisoning years fall away.
My heart grows resonant
with the unforgettable echo of released joy.

ODE FOR A SUMMER DAY

On an afternoon toward July's end
we wandered at random through a forest
some of us could remember
before it became really used to people.

We came to a meadow that might have been Greece,
but was not.
The flowers might have been asphodels
in another time and place,
but this was New Mexico, not Greece
and had its own myths
and its own reality.

Above us Tsikomo Mountain
was involved in a mystery of cloud
held holy still by only a few old men
yet shedding a certain radiance
hard to explain in reasonable terms.
The mountain was rich with the energy of summer:
tall grass bending in the light wind,
cranesbill and harebells daring to bloom together
in a delicate dissonance of mauve and sea-blue.

Then suddenly music
unexpected in this remnant of wilderness
where red penstemon bloomed like wands on the cooled lavas,
reminder of ancient fires.
Young hikers came out of the distance with recorders;
then a woman who carried mariposa lilies
and wove them in her hair.
They smiled upon us as though just strayed
from some antique ritual of summer.
Our hearts rippled in joyful recognition.

We took our own way then
and crossed the stream into a blossomy meadow
almost Elysian.
There were aspens waving a magic circle round us,
bright-stemmed among the dark firs.

A visual music
took form on the mirror of our eyes.
We seemed to move in a design of dancers,
hands clasped or
now and then parted in figures of separation.
Woven in and out of shadow
as whatever music we were part of filled us
we heard the voiceless mountain
speak;
the wordless water
listened in the coil of our ears
to its own singing.

Remember forever the frolic of dogs and children,
the mushrooms we gathered
and trusted not to harm us,
birdsong invisible as angels,
beavers which dreamed us like men,
or was it we through whose dream the beavers glided
in their swamplike Paradise?

Coming on water hemlock
that lifted its lace of flowers in a white embroidery
out of the muck-black soil
we heard ourselves speaking of death
and of Socrates.
One of the children
discovered a rat's sharp skull,
carried it with her
the rest of the afternoon.
None overheard
what her questioning fingers told her.

A horse's rough bones
lay inarticulate and random
on the deep forest floor.
Was it an eagle watched us
from the lightning-blasted fir?
Death moved among us like the blindfold figure
in an old children's game.
His hand was not yet lifted.

Remember forever,
holding our breaths as we watched,
a small girl walking a fallen branch across the black bog
toward her father's reaching hand.
She became all of us
for a transfigured moment,
the child in us all
crossing the dark abyss on a cobweb strand.
Our hearts and our indrawn breaths upheld her.
Invisible music beat like wings among us.

Trembling so on the verge of ecstasy
was it our laughter kept us safely human?
Hands reaching out to touch,
the minds and the hearts met,
the calls heard by the far one in the wood
"Where are you?"

Where were we? Where had we been?
What magical summoning
brought us together with this day
and made us dancers
in an antique rite of summer?
The timeless moment
held us and let us go.
The music lingered
for a long while among us.
Why does my heart still tremble
at the sound of a falling leaf?

LINES FOR A GRANDDAUGHTER, AGE TWENTY

I sit across from you at the morning table;
the birds fly in quick wreaths outside the window
and the snow is limned with the shadow of winter branches.
We are two women who have come here today to share life
across a barrier
that only birds can cross
or thoughts like birds
free to the mutual air.
It is time that holds us
too far apart for touch,
time wide as a continent
or as the space through which light travels
from one star to another.

I look at you as sorrowing Demeter
must have looked at her straying child, Persephone,
as at her own lost youth.
The rift of separation
is wide between us.
I have been part of
a time that is long gone by;
your time has not yet
ripened its memory.
You travel ahead of me,
younger than I and yet much wiser;
the trees of life grow taller
as the generations pass.
How can I show you
what my own spring was like?

Our journeys bring us together at a crossroad
where you must go one way and I another.
The maps I have made will have no meaning for you;
the landmarks are not the same.
You will be traveling in a different season
by a path that must be your own.
My own way now leads downward
like the winter's leaf
toward death and dissolution.
What is there I can leave you
but a moment's glimpse of the rainbow
the setting sun casts at evening
on the last cloud?

PERHAPS IN OUR OLD AGE

Perhaps in our old age
we can return again to being children,
return to our playful places,
to the magic world we were once part of:
to the roots of old trees where the gnomes delved
and hid their secret treasure;
to the fairy wand that could transform us;
to the finger dipped in the cauldron
and the language of birds understood then;
to the shoes of swiftness and the cap of darkness;
to the game of horse thieves;
to Dapplegrim our great steed
who helped the lad win a kingdom
and a princess;
to the well where the maiden dropped her spindle
and fell after it into a fairy realm.
Perhaps in our old age
we can find that well again and lean above it
and behold our own long lost treasure.

Let us unearth our childhood
like a bone hidden and long forgotten
by an old dog, and gnaw the marrow of it
and bring the taste back again
of those times when our imaginations ran free
and every straight stick became a pony
and our real ponies steeds of fire.
Let us take hands and reenter the loved stories
as though we were children running from a schoolroom
into a world we long ago lost and longed for,
that waits for us still at the far edge of dreaming;
a world where the wicked witch is at last outwitted,
where the shining birch tree
drops gold and silver blessings on the true bride.

CONVOCATION OF BLUEBIRDS

The day flickered with bluebirds.
Blue flames swirled upward
again and again out of the green tree.
The dull-coated robins
withdrew
each posting himself like a baffled officer
at the edge of a demonstration,
a demonstration of light incarnate in blue feathers,
motion of blue dancers,
splintered fragments of blue sky.

What focus of energy drew them
again and again to the one tree
that seemed no different from the scrubby others,
compacting them inward like a dark star,
then all at once hurling them outward
in a burst of blue fireworks,
a fountain of slant feathers,
a scatter of blue sparks flying
every which way against the bare sky?

What did they celebrate?
What wordless convocation drew them
out of winter silence into this wilderness,
to make a barren tree blossom,
to ripple the sky with a blue wind,
to proclaim the advent of spring among the mesas?

What gods walked with their headdress of sky among us?
The stolid robins,
blind to epiphanies, made insulted comments;
each separate, jealous of territory
defended his own outpost
against gods or whatever comers.
Only we humans
felt our hearts tremble as we watched,
sharing some mystery long ago forgotten.

THE KITES AND THE PETROGLYPHS

A medley of children
and a melody of kites
on this February afternoon.
The air
a hemisphere of blue light,
radiant light;
the kites streamed in it
like tadpoles in a millpond,
slender and serpentine,
colored rose red,
colored purple;
one butterfly fluttering;
one with a little tail that twinkled
like a caught star dipped in silver.

It seemed like an odd place to fly kites—
thirty miles more or less from anywhere
at the tip of a blunt-finned ridge of lava
cutting the cliff-rimmed plain in two.
We had to crawl through
a tight-strung barbwire fence to get there,
meant to keep cattle in and intruders out.
We knew we were trespassing but
the place had been ceremonial
long before cattle and fences.
Ancient holy creatures were glyphed into the smooth rock,
Sky Beings had been invoked with power here.

Had our timing been right by chance
or had we perhaps been summoned
by spirits tired of long-sleeping
to hold our feast here,
a little festival of stringed kites
that looped and spun in the bright air?

Among their stars and serpents
we sent our own;
we became children with our children
for the space of an afternoon,
fulfilled, filled full of light.
The ancient Beings seemed to laugh with us.
Old Kokopelli
hunched on his sun-warmed rock
lifted his fertile flute and smiled too.

FOR A MOUNTAIN BURIAL

A granite ridge:
the mountain's firm crust
once fluid
become stone.
We buried her
under the low-bending branch of a fir tree,
all that was left
after the final burning,
her bodily remains
reduced as much as possible
to ash.

Some of it drifted in a fine veil
on the light cloudy wind;
the rest we mingled
with granite particles
and leaf-mold,
and I thought of the tree
drawing its mineral nourishment
from bone cells
and crumbled granite.

Let rain's dark music
dissolve her elements;
we leave her to the mountain mists and waters,
forgetting the long struggle not to die,
cleansing our memories
of the last traces of possession.
Let no one now strive to keep her
captive to any mind
or heart-formed image.
May all ghosts take the form of birds
and begin singing
among the birds of daybreak.